KT-385-354

Mad about...

# Bugs

written by Deborah Murrell
illustrated by Ian Escott

consultant: Stuart Hine, Department of Entomology,
The Natural History Museum.

A catalogue record for this book is available from the British Library

Published by Ladybird Books Ltd
80 Strand London WC2R 0RL
A Penguin Company

015
© LADYBIRD BOOKS LTD MMVIII
LADYBIRD and the device of a Ladybird are trademarks of Ladybird Books Ltd

ISBN-13: 978 1 84646 801 8

Printed in China

# Contents

Some words appear in **bold** in this book.
Turn to the glossary to learn about them.

# What are bugs?

We use the word bugs to mean a large number of small animals. The term can include **insects** of all kinds, spiders and scorpions, centipedes and millipedes, and sometimes worms, slugs and snails. Bugs are divided into groups according to the number of legs they have.

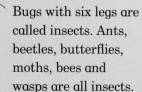

Bugs with six legs are called insects. Ants, beetles, butterflies, moths, bees and wasps are all insects.

Spiders and scorpions
are called **arachnids**.
They have eight legs.
Mites and ticks are
also arachnids.

Centipedes and millipedes have
more than eight legs. Although their
names mean 'one hundred feet' and
'one thousand feet', some centipedes
have more than 300 legs, and
millipedes can have as few as 24.

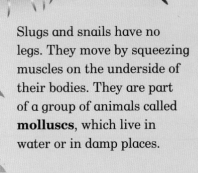

Slugs and snails have no
legs. They move by squeezing
muscles on the underside of
their bodies. They are part
of a group of animals called
**molluscs**, which live in
water or in damp places.

# Bug bodies

Both insects and arachnids have an **exoskeleton**, which is a hard covering on the outside of their bodies. This both protects them and holds their bodies together.

wing

Wasps are typical insects. Their bodies are divided into three distinct areas; the head, **thorax** and **abdomen**. Unlike us, they have no skeleton inside their bodies.

abdomen

Snails have soft bodies, which are protected by their shells. Their shells grow with them.

tentacle

eye

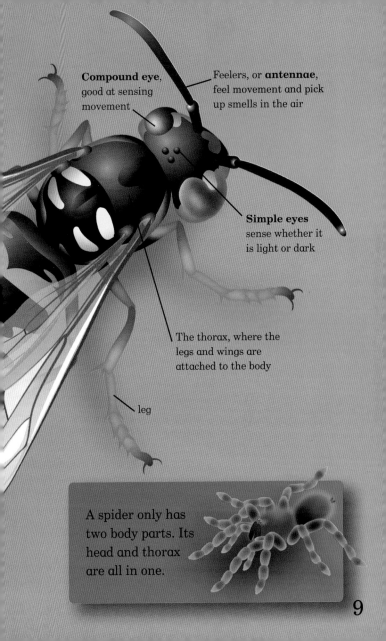

**Compound eye**, good at sensing movement

Feelers, or **antennae**, feel movement and pick up smells in the air

**Simple eyes** sense whether it is light or dark

The thorax, where the legs and wings are attached to the body

leg

A spider only has two body parts. Its head and thorax are all in one.

9

# A bug's life

Bugs eat all kinds of food. Many insects feed on plants, but others hunt and kill other animals for food. These are called **predators**.

Some wasps and scorpions use their sting to kill or paralyse their **prey**.

Death stalker scorpion, the most poisonous scorpion on Earth

Different kinds of bugs have different life cycles.

Female scorpions, like this emperor scorpion, give birth to live young. They keep their young safe by carrying the babies on their backs.

## The life cycle of a butterfly

**1** Female butterflies lay eggs.

**2** A **larva** hatches out of the egg.

**3** The larva changes into a **pupa**.

**4** Eventually, a butterfly comes out of the pupa.

Snails lay eggs, out of which young snails hatch.

11

# How they move

Bugs have many different ways of getting around. Most of them can walk or crawl, but some also jump, fly or swim.

The front legs of a water boatman look rather like oars. It uses them to paddle around in ponds and lakes.

Ladybirds can both walk and fly. You can often see them on plants, eating **aphids**.

Grasshoppers and crickets are great jumpers. A large grasshopper can jump more than one metre in a single leap!

Centipedes and millipedes have many legs and both are fast movers. Some can cover 50 centimetres in a single second. If they lose a leg, another one will grow in its place.

If you have a computer, you can download a poster of different bugs from www.ladybird.com/madabout

Butterflies have two pairs of wings, which they use to fly from flower to flower, feeding on **nectar**.

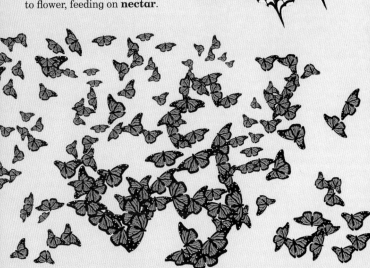

Some monarch butterflies fly thousands of miles between North and South America, to avoid the cold North American winter.

# Bugs in water

Ponds are full of bugs, especially in spring and summer, when animals begin to have their young.

Frogs lay hundreds of eggs, or frogspawn, in the water, though only a few will grow to be adult frogs. Eggs, **tadpoles** and young frogs are eaten by many animals.

Diving beetles are fierce predators. They feed on tadpoles, worms, small fish and insects.

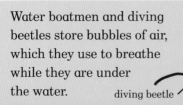

Water boatmen and diving beetles store bubbles of air, which they use to breathe while they are under the water.

diving beetle

Dragonflies often bring a flash of colour to ponds and lakes in the summer. They feed on other flying insects that they catch in mid-air.

Pond skaters live on the surface of water, eating insects that fall in. Special hairs on their feet allow them to stand on the water's surface without falling in themselves.

15

# Bugs in the air

Beetles have tough front wings that they use only as wing cases. These protect their flight wings when they are not flying. Other insects simply fold their wings away.

Most insects have two pairs of wings.

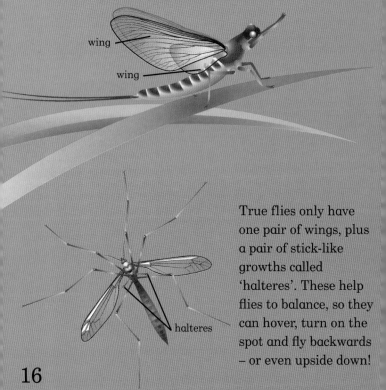

wing

wing

True flies only have one pair of wings, plus a pair of stick-like growths called 'halteres'. These help flies to balance, so they can hover, turn on the spot and fly backwards – or even upside down!

halteres

House flies taste food with their feet. That's how they know when they've landed on something good to eat! They cover the food in spit, which makes it turn to a liquid, like soup, and then suck it all up.

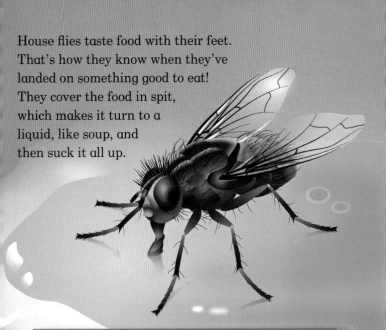

You can usually tell the difference between a moth and a butterfly by looking at their antennae. Most moths have feathery-looking or thread-like antennae, but butterfly antennae have small knobs at the end. Butterflies fly during the day, and moths mostly fly at night.

butterfly antennae

moth antennae

17

# Bugs underground

Certain types of bugs live under the ground. Some dig **burrows** to lay their eggs in, and then the young have to dig to the surface when they hatch. Others use burrows to hunt their prey.

Earthworms are good at keeping the soil healthy. As they move through soil, they take some in through their mouths at the head end and then pass the undigested soil out at the other end. This mixes the layers of soil and allows water and air to get into it.

Trapdoor spiders use their **fangs** to dig into the ground. They make a 'trapdoor' out of silk and mud to cover the entrance. When an insect comes by, the spider jumps out and grabs it!

The mole cricket digs a burrow with its shovel-shaped front legs. In the breeding season the male cricket sings to attract a female at the burrow entrance. The entrance of the burrow is specially shaped so the sound carries for more than a kilometre.

19

# Bugs on land

Most bugs spend some time on or above the ground. Some bugs are brightly coloured, which may be a warning to other animals that they don't taste good. Others blend perfectly into their backgrounds, and can hide from predators and prey alike.

Dung beetles eat the dung of other animals. Some females roll dung into a big ball, into which they lay their eggs. When the young are born, they don't have far to go for their first meal!

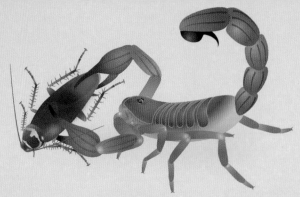

Scorpions rest under rocks in daytime and come out to hunt for insects and other small animals at night.

Stag beetles got their name because their enormous jaws look like the antlers of a stag. Male stag beetles use theirs to fight.

Tarantulas are spiders that do not make webs to catch their prey, but hunt on the ground. Some are large enough to prey on birds and small **mammals**.

21

Millipedes live under rocks, logs or leaves. They mainly come out at night. If a millipede senses danger, it curls up so that its head and soft underbelly are protected.

Praying mantids get their name from the way they hold their front legs – they look as if they are praying.

front legs

leg spikes

This bug can look almost invisible against a green leaf or plant stalk. When its prey gets too close, its front legs whip out and the spikes hold the prey still while the mantis begins to eat!

Fireflies are actually beetles. Most fireflies can produce light at the end of their abdomens. They use the light at night to attract a mate.

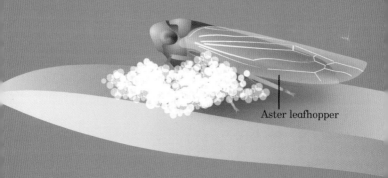

Aster leafhopper

Leafhoppers live on plants and trees. They make the white foam that is sometimes called 'cuckoo spit' by blowing air into plant **sap**. This helps to hide them from predators while they feed on more of the sap.

23

# Bug societies

Some bugs live in big social groups, called colonies. They look after each other and their young, too. Termite and ant colonies can contain several million bugs, all usually ruled by one queen, a female who lays all the eggs.

giant termite nest

Termites can build huge nests. Often the nests have a sort of chimney built into them that keeps them cool. Warm air rises and flows out the top of the chimney. This draws in cooler air through holes in the side of the nest.

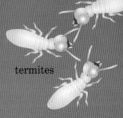

termites

Bee colonies are made up of female worker bees, who build and defend the nest. One queen lays all the eggs. Once a year, some males are born. They mate with the queen and then die.

Bees make their food from the nectar of flowers. When a bee finds nectar, it returns to the nest and dances for the other bees. The shape of the dance tells the bees how far away the flowers are and in which direction.

# Fantastic factfile

sucking mouth part

- Scientists use the term 'true bugs' to mean a group of insects with a sucking mouth part, which they use for feeding. Other insects do not have sucking mouth parts.

- Some dung beetles are incredibly strong. They can move a ball of dung almost fifty times their own weight.

- A honeybee can only sting once. When it does, it leaves its sting behind, and it soon dies.

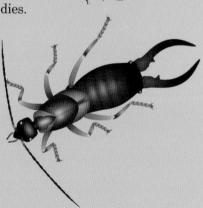

- Earwigs got their name because people once believed they crawled into their ears when they were asleep. This isn't true.

- Butterflies and moths are found in all parts of the world except Antarctica.

- People once used spiders' webs to bandage cuts. The webs contain a natural antiseptic, which can help to stop infection.

- A cockroach can live without a head for at least a week. It will only eventually die because it can't eat or drink.

- Some wasps lay their eggs inside other animals, such as spiders, caterpillars or other insects. When the eggs hatch, the young wasps eat the animal from the inside out!

- Dragonflies have existed for millions of years. They were around even before the dinosaurs! The largest prehistoric dragonfly had a wingspan of 60 centimetres across, while the biggest today has a wingspan of only 19 centimetres.

# Amazing bug awards

## Fastest

The emperor dragonfly can fly at almost one hundred kilometres per hour! That's almost as fast as the motorway speed limit in most countries.

## Loudest

The loudest insect is the male African cicada. Its buzzing call can be heard up to 400 metres away.

## Heaviest

The heaviest insect is the goliath beetle. A large beetle can weigh up to 100 grams, which is about the same as an average apple.

## ⭐ Smallest

Fairyflies are the smallest insects, although they are not actually flies, but small wasps. They are only 0.2 millimetres long, about the size of a pinhead.

## ⭐ Biggest

The largest land snail is the Giant African snail. It can measure up to 40 centimetres long. That's about the same size as a guinea pig!

## ⭐ Strongest web

Orb-web spiders make the biggest, strongest webs. They may be up to two metres wide, and are strong enough to trap small birds.

# Glossary

**abdomen** – the third and lower part of an insect's body, containing the guts and reproductive organs.

**antennae** – a pair of feelers on an insect's head used for sensing smells and movement.

**aphid** – a tiny insect that feeds on the sap from plants.

**arachnid** – an animal with an exoskeleton and eight legs, such as a spider or scorpion.

**burrow** – the underground home of some animals.

**compound eye** – an eye with many different surfaces that is good at sensing movement.

**exoskeleton** – a hard shell or outer covering that protects and supports the bodies of some insects.

**fangs** – large, sharp needles, which some animals use to inject poison.

**insect** – an animal with an exoskeleton, six legs and three body sections, such as an ant.

**larva** – the stage after hatching from eggs, before some insects change into their adult form.

**mammal** – an animal with a backbone and hair or fur, that usually gives birth to live young.

**mollusc** – an animal with a soft body and usually a shell.

**nectar** – a sweet, sugary liquid found in flowers, on which many insects such as bees and butterflies feed.

**predator** – an animal that hunts and eats other animals.

**prey** – an animal that is eaten by other animals.

**pupa** – a stage that some insects go through between larva and their adult form.

**sap** – the liquid inside a plant.

**simple eye** – an eye with a single lens that can only sense light or dark.

**tadpole** – the larva of frogs or toads.

**thorax** – the middle part of an insect's body where the legs and wings are attached.